Intersections:
Where Faith and Life Meet

A Cumberland Presbyterian
Adult Resource
Volume 12, Prayer

FAITH
F
E

Discipleship Ministry Team
Ministry Council
Cumberland Presbyterian Church

8207 Traditional Place
Cordova, Tennessee 38016

First Edition 2016

Published by The Discipleship Ministry Team
General Assembly Ministry Council of the Cumberland Presbyterian Church
Cordova, Tennessee

ISBN-13: 978-0692566251

ISBN-10: 0692566252

We want to hear from you.
Please send your comments about this curriculum to
the Discipleship Ministry Team at chm@cumberland.org

OUR UNITED OUTREACH
Made Possible In Part By Your Tithe To Our United Outreach

Table of Contents

Lesson 1   What Do You Do with a Drunken Woman? 4

Lesson 2   The Dark Night of the Soul 13

Lesson 3   What to Do When Worship Stinks 23

Lesson 4   Words to Live By 33

Lesson 5   Bootstrap Religion 42

Lesson 6   Isn't That Just Like a Woman? 51

Lesson 7   Eyes Wide Shut 60

Editor: Cindy Martin
Proofreader: Marsha Hudson

To order, call 901-276-4572, x 252 or e-mail resources@cumberland.org.

What Do You Do with a Drunken Woman?

Scripture for lesson: 1 Samuel 1:9-20

Let us open this lesson on prayer with these words from the hymn "Open My Eyes, That I May See" written by Clara H. Scott in 1895.

Open my eyes, that I may see
Glimpses of truth Thou hast for me;
Place in my hands the wonderful key
That shall unclasp and set me free.
Chorus
Silently now I wait for Thee,
Ready my God, Thy will to see,
Open my eyes, illumine me,
Spirit divine!

When I was a child I went to bed every night with one prayer on my lips: "Dear God, make me a redhead." I wanted more than anything to have beautiful red hair. I would have settled for auburn, but I wanted red. Yet every morning when I woke up I had the same ash blonde hair I'd always had. As I grew, my prayer changed to asking God to give me at least one redheaded child. Three children later, three more blondes! How could it be that something I prayed for so much, wanted so badly, never happened?

The truth of the matter is that what I was doing was much more like wishing than praying. If everyone's wishes came true, there would be a huge over-population of ponies and puppies! Too often we treat prayers like wishes, little petitions lifted up to God's ears that we hope will be answered with great speed and very little effort on our part. Such wishes are far distant and at least twice-removed cousins from true prayer. They bear little, if any, resemblance to what prayers from a faithful person should be.

How does prayer open your eyes? How does it set you free?

For what have you prayed that God didn't answer in the way you asked? How have you handled your disappointment?

What makes something a prayer instead of a wish? How do you make that distinction for yourself? for the church?

Prep for the Journey

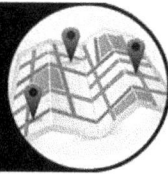

While wandering in the wilderness with Moses, the people of Israel received instructions from God for creating a tabernacle. Because the people were nomads, it was essential that their place of worship be portable. Once the people entered the Promised Land, they erected the tabernacle at Shiloh. It remained at Shiloh until King David moved the center of worship to Jerusalem where he built a tabernacle in which to place the Ark of the Covenant. Solomon later built the first permanent dwelling place for God.

First Samuel tells us about a woman who prayed so fervently at Shiloh that the priest thought she must surely be drunk. Shiloh became associated so strongly with prayer that people still go to the site of the archaeological dig to pray.

On the Road

In our scripture for this lesson we find a woman named Hannah who, despite all of the things stacked against her, prayed to God for a son. Scripture tells us that Hannah's husband, Elkanah, loved her very much. However, Hannah was barren, which was a grave issue for women in biblical times. Not only was barrenness thought to be an indication of sin against God, but a great deal of a woman's identity and worth centered on being a mother, specifically a mother of boys.

Hannah lived with her husband and his other wife, Peninnah, whose sons and daughters were daily reminders of Hannah's closed womb. It didn't help matters any that Peninnah regularly provoked Hannah over her inability to have children. When the family was observing an annual festival at the tabernacle in Shiloh, Hannah decided that she had had enough.

Read 1 Samuel 1:9-11.

After they had eaten and drunk at Shiloh, Hannah rose and presented herself before the LORD. Now Eli the priest was sitting on the seat beside the doorpost of the temple of the LORD. ¹⁰ She was deeply distressed and prayed to the LORD, and wept bitterly. ¹¹ She made this vow: "O LORD of hosts, if only you will look on the misery of your servant, and remember me, and not forget your servant, but will give to your servant a male child, then I will set him before you as a Nazirite until the day of his death. He shall drink neither wine nor intoxicants, and no razor shall touch his head."

Many important things happened at Shiloh. Use a concordance or Bible dictionary to learn about them.

How have you handled being provoked? Were your responses appropriate? If not, what responses might have been better?

5

When have you set aside religious conventions and gone to God without any prescribed rules or approved words? What happened? How did the experience change you?

When have you witnessed others bargaining with God? When have you struck such a deal yourself? What is the difference between making a deal with God and offering a way of serving God? List some examples.

Elkanah and his family made annual trips to Shiloh where they offered sacrifices to God. Eli and his sons served as priests for the tabernacle at Shiloh.

Whenever they visited Shiloh, Peninnah's harassment of Hannah increased to the point that Hannah was so distressed she was unable to eat. After one such occasion, Hannah went into the tabernacle to have a one-on-one conversation with God. What an amazingly brave thing to do! She boldly went before the throne of God and placed her heart's desire at God's feet, not bothering to go through her husband or even through a priest. She sought God on her own and asked God to intervene in her life in a very real way.

Hannah bared her soul to God. She truly believed that God would hear and answer her prayer. Hannah had a relationship with God, not as her husband's God or her tribal God, but as her personal God. Her pain and suffering were real, whether they were caused by the deep need for a son or the rejection she felt in a world that condemned her for being barren. She went to God in the purest way, giving herself into God's hands.

Hannah promised that if God gave her a son, she would raise the child as a Nazirite. Normally a Nazirite vow was taken only for a specific period of time, but Hannah vowed that her son would be a Nazarite from birth and would be set apart for God's service.

Many people think Hannah was bargaining with God—a "you scratch my back and I'll scratch yours" kind of promise. Personally, I think Hannah, in the emptiness of her soul, was so drawn to God that she was willing to give up everything, even the child she so desperately sought, in order to be made whole by God. Her prayer was not an offer of quid pro quo, but an honest reflection of her faith.

Scenic Route

Hannah's story is held up as one of hope, of promises made and fulfilled. But there is a point in the story when the reader thinks it may not come to pass, where Hannah's actions seem to have been for naught. The religious leader of the day was not too keen on her interaction with God.

Read 1 Samuel 1:12-14.

As she continued praying before the LORD, Eli observed her mouth. [13] Hannah was praying silently; only her lips moved, but her voice was not heard; therefore Eli thought she was drunk. [14] So Eli said to her, "How long will you make a drunken spectacle of yourself? Put away your wine."

Enter Eli, the head priest, who took exception to Hannah's way of praying. The fact that he could not hear her words and that she had ignored the proper rules and procedures for addressing God did not sit well with Eli. In his mind, the only explanation for her behavior was that she had over-indulged in wine and was drunk at the foot of the altar.

Eli was tasked with helping the people of Israel worship God and follow God's ways, which Hannah clearly was not doing. He railed against her, claiming that she was not only out of line, but intoxicated as well. Eli felt that her behavior could push God's blessing out of the tabernacle. God was doing a new thing through Hannah, one that would change the course of Israel's history, but Eli was circumspect of her reasoning, method, and motive.

Workers Ahead — CAUTION

Hannah, luckily, refused to be ashamed of addressing the Lord so boldly. In fact she cried out to the priest to correct his misconception. She had entered the tabernacle with an earnest desire to meet God and poured out herself as an offering.

Read 1 Samuel 1:15-17.

But Hannah answered, "No, my lord, I am a woman deeply troubled; I have drunk neither wine nor strong drink, but I have been pouring out my soul before the LORD. [16] Do not regard your servant as a worthless woman, for I have been speaking out of my great anxiety and vexation all this time." [17] Then Eli answered, "Go in peace; the God of Israel grant the petition you have made to him."

Once again, Hannah's boldness surprised Eli. She had gumption! Eli blessed her and sent her on her way. Perhaps Eli was ready to get her out of the tabernacle, or perhaps he saw evidence of a genuine encounter with the Lord God on her face. Whatever the case, it seems clear from the text that Hannah had a real interaction with God. She sought God's blessing the best way she knew how and left with a different outlook on her life.

Hannah left that place a changed woman. Verse 18 tells us "And she said, "Let your servant find favor in your sight." Then the woman went to her quarters, ate and drank with her husband, and her countenance was sad no longer." Her conversation with God had changed Hannah. She was no longer depressed and despairing. She left with a heart uplifted and was able to join her family in their celebration.

Prayer changes us. Many of us have heard this statement, but until it happens to us we are afraid to admit the truth in those words. Hannah left with a lightened spirit. She didn't leave pregnant. She didn't

When have you questioned the way another Christian addressed God? What about that situation made you uncomfortable? How did you handle it? How could you have responded differently and still been faithful to your beliefs?

When have you had a real encounter with God? How did the experience change you?

How has prayer changed you? How have you seen prayer change others? How does God's response to prayer affect you? other people? How can the church pray in ways that are life-changing?

Who taught you how to pray? What lessons did you learn? What lesson do you wish you had learned?

leave with the sure knowledge that God would open her womb. But she did leave knowing that she had placed her whole soul before God and entrusted her life into the Lord's capable hands.

Many people, probably even people in your group or congregation, can testify to the power of prayer and how it has changed their lives. Being willing to share what God is doing and has done is important in our spiritual formation and the discipleship of others. In order to share what God is doing, we must be able to identify God's activity in our lives.

I have struggled with teaching my children to pray. I want them to pray like Hannah, with honesty and openness before God, but at three years old that is difficult. It doesn't get much easier at 7 and 11 years old. So my husband and I taught them prayers to say and lines to memorize, as a way to get used to talking with God. When they go "off script" I don't correct them. I encourage them to express to God what they are thinking and feeling, and to trust that God will listen to any words from their hearts.

In the Rear View

In time, scripture tells us, Hannah conceived and bore a son. Because of her daring and boldness in prayer, her life was changed forever. It was changed not just because she bore a child, but because she trusted completely in God's will and presence in her life.

It is so powerful to watch someone who really believes God is listening to him or her pray. The space becomes alive with electricity, and you cannot imagine anyone other than the living God listening intently. The openness and honesty of such a prayer is a blessing to all who hear it. May our prayers be of the same substance as Hannah's prayer. May we be open to the leading of God's Holy Spirit in all that we do, even when convention may tell us otherwise. May we pray prayers that change us, and by changing us, change the world in which we live and serve.

Take a moment to lift up your concerns and needs before God and one another. Pray as a group or by dividing into prayer partners. Covenant to lift up one another through prayer in the week to come.

When do you feel God's presence most often? How willing are you to be as open and honest with God as Hannah was?

Travel Log

Day 1:

Read again the opening stanza of "Open My Eyes, That I May see" from the beginning of this lesson. What are the glimpses of truth God has for you today? Where would God have you share those words of truth with others? Jot down some of your thoughts below.

Day 2:

How do you normally pray? Do you organize your prayers or are they more free-flowing? Today write out your prayers as if you were writing a letter to God. Don't leave anything out; don't hold back. Offer yourself freely to your Lord.

Day 3:

Read over the letter you wrote to God yesterday. What things have you learned since writing it? What answers have you received? How are you different today than when you wrote those words? Journal about your thoughts and feelings regarding the prayer and what you have learned.

Take time to pray again today for things that are still unclear to you.

Day 4:

Change your posture for prayer. If you normally sit to pray, try standing or kneeling. If you normally kneel to pray, try lying down. If you are still, try moving. Our prayers often change when we change our way of doing them. Be intentional about this change.

Day 5:

Think back to your prayer time yesterday. How did you change your prayer time? What benefits did you notice? What was uncomfortable? What might you be willing to try again? How did you hear God's voice? Make some notes as to the differences you experienced through these changes.

Day 6:

Poetry and song lyrics are often someone's prayers that were written down. Try focusing your prayers by using one of the following suggestions: Create an acrostic poem (the beginning letter of each line spells a word such as: PRAYER, BOLDLY, CHANGE, or HOPE) or write a Haiku poem (a Japanese poem of seventeen syllables, in three lines of five, seven, and five, traditionally evoking images of the natural world). If the thought of writing poetry overwhelms you, just note some words that you associate with prayer.

Day 7:

    People often pray the most during times of anxiety and stress. How can you commit to having an attitude and practice of prayer that goes beyond crisis mode and into a daily discipline? Make notes about your schedule and the places where you can make adjustments to allow for time dedicated to prayer. Try these options and select one that works well for you. Commit to this prayer time for the duration of this Bible study.

The Dark Night Of the Soul

Scripture for the lesson: Job 1:1-3, 6-12; 6:8-13; 19:25; 42:1-6

Let us open this lesson on prayer with the second verse from the hymn "Open My Eyes, That I May See," written by Clara H. Scott in 1895.

Open my ears, that I may hear
Voices of truth Thou sendest clear;
And while the wave notes fall on my ear,
Everything false will disappear.
Chorus
Silently now I wait for Thee,
Ready my God, Thy will to see,
Open my ears, illumine me,
Spirit divine!

One afternoon, not too long ago, my seven-year-old daughter came into the room with tears pouring down her face. She looked up at me and then threw herself on the floor crying, wailing, "My life is over! Why am I still breathing?" She had been in an argument with her friend, and the friend had told her she was no longer her "best" best friend. My young daughter couldn't imagine anything hurting more than the pain she felt at that moment. She was in the depths of despair and did not understand why her body kept breathing when her spirit was crushed.

Prep for the Journey

In the Old Testament, people thought God's favor was bestowed on people in the form of blessings such as children (remember Hannah) and wealth. Job was such a man. He had large flocks and many children, plus he was known to be righteous.

When have you felt crushed? When have you thought that you were suffering more than you could possibly endure? What did you do?

What attitudes and thoughts do you bring to the story of Job? What have you heard about this man of faith?

What do you think about God and Satan having such a conversation? Why?

If God and Satan had a conversation about you, what might be said?

Read Job 1:1-3.

There was once a man in the land of Uz whose name was Job. That man was blameless and upright, one who feared God and turned away from evil. ² *There were born to him seven sons and three daughters.* ³ *He had seven thousand sheep, three thousand camels, five hundred yoke of oxen, five hundred donkeys, and very many servants; so that this man was the greatest of all the people of the east.*

The book that bears his name tells the tale of Job's suffering. Through no fault of his own, Job lost EVERYTHING—children, flocks, material possessions, and even his own health. In this odd story, the reader follows as Job was torn apart by suffering, pain, and loss.

On the Road

The very unique biblical account of Job tells us that God and Satan were having a conversation. At that time, Satan was not a proper name, but referred to one who instigated evil on the earth. Therefore, it was natural that God would ask Satan for an accounting of his whereabouts. Satan's answer was akin to a teenager's response of "just hanging out."

Read Job 1:6-8.

One day the heavenly beings came to present themselves before the LORD, and Satan also came among them. ⁷ *The LORD said to Satan, "Where have you come from?" Satan answered the LORD, "From going to and fro on the earth, and from walking up and down on it."* ⁸ *The LORD said to Satan, "Have you considered my servant Job? There is no one like him on the earth, a blameless and upright man who fears God and turns away from evil."*

It almost feels like something is missing at this point. Why did God go straight from asking about Satan's whereabouts to asking if Satan had considered Job? Maybe Satan had said something about a lack of faithfulness among God's people. Then it's almost as if God was bragging by asking Satan if he had considered Job, who was righteous and blameless. Satan scoffed at God's suggestion, claiming that Job was only faithful because God had been protecting and blessing him. Without God's blessings, Satan felt sure that Job would quickly lose his faith. So, God allowed Job to be put to the test.

Read Job 1:9-12.

Then Satan answered the LORD, "Does Job fear God for nothing? ¹⁰ *Have you not put a fence around him and his house and all that he has, on every side? You have blessed the work of his hands, and his posses-sions have increased in the land. ¹¹ But stretch out your hand now, and touch all that he has, and he will curse you to your face." ¹² The LORD said to Satan, "Very well, all that he has is in your power; only do not stretch out your hand against him!" So Satan went out from the pres-ence of the LORD.*

I must admit that the way this book begins disturbs me. Why were God and Satan having a casual conversation in heaven? Why was God attempting to convince Satan of anything? I am disturbed by the idea that God might move the hand of protection from the faith-ful in order to "test" them. I am upset by the way Job seemed to have been nothing more than a pawn in a game between God and Satan.

With these "anti-Job" thoughts, I often want to bypass this book. But it is in the scriptures, so we read it and hope to find God's truth in its story.

Disaster after disaster soon struck Job and his household. His children were killed when a wind caused their house to collapse onto them. Raiders stole his livestock and killed his servants. Job had noth-ing left, but he remained faithful to God. However, it was natural that his friends, and even his wife, would question what he had done to earn God's disfavor.

In the passage for today we find ourselves in the early part of Job's prayer, Job's confession. And we see a side of prayer not often taught by the church or modeled by our congregations.

Read Job 6:8-10.

"O that I might have my request,
and that God would grant my desire;
⁹ that it would please God to crush me,
that he would let loose his hand and cut me off!
¹⁰ This would be my consolation;
I would even exult in unrelenting pain;
for I have not denied the words of the Holy One."

Job was ready to give up. He had had enough of the suffering and pain. He boldly cried out that he wished God would just cut him off. He begged God to crush him. These are words of pain, suffering, and anger. These words are not ones we often hear in church, where the focus is more on healing and hope. Yet here they sit as a model of prayer.

The grief Job expressed resonates with many of us. The night after my grandma's death, my mother roamed the halls of our home, wailing at God. She begged God to end her suffering. She could not bear any more loss or pain. I remember lying in my bed, getting very upset, and finally coming out of my room to tell her to stop yelling. I told her that she was not the only one in the house who was grieving, and that her actions were making things harder for the rest of us.

I can't begin to tell you how many times I have wished I could take those words back. My 19-year-old self had no way of under-

What parts of the story of Job bother you? How do the bother-some parts affect your reading of the story?

Why can we cry out to God in our deepest despair and loss? How can we be as honest as Job about our frustrations and perceived injustices?

15

When have you not allowed someone to voice his or her grief or anger to God, or at God? When has someone stopped you from this kind of expression? How did it affect your relationship with God?

How do you feel knowing that God is with you even when things are difficult? When have you railed against God? How important is it to you that God can handle your railing and not abandon you?

standing the pain and loss a child would feel when a parent dies. I couldn't see past my own grief to realize that Mom's crying out was a legitimate way of voicing her heart's earnest prayer to God. I did not take the time to see God present even in my Mom's frightening grief. Instead I acted more like Job's wife, who eventually told him to curse God and die.

Scenic Route

Job could see no reason for his suffering and so continued to cry out that it be ended. Job did not deny the existence of God, nor did he claim that God was not in control. He just asked God to stop his suffering and pain.

Read Job 6:11-13.

What is my strength, that I should wait?
    And what is my end, that I should be patient?
[12] Is my strength the strength of stones,
    or is my flesh bronze?
[13] In truth I have no help in me,
    and any resource is driven from me.

These verses are perhaps one of the most honest and open confessions about humanity that we find in scripture. Job was admitting his powerlessness against the things happening around him. There were no resources within his grasp that could change or make sense of the calamities that had befallen him. Nothing he could do would restore his wealth, his property, or his children. He was very much aware of his position in the world. But he cried out to God. Why?

Job knew that he was not the one ultimately in charge. Job cried out to God, trusting that his grievances would be heard. He cried out to God, trusting that even in the darkest moment he could imagine, God had not abandoned him.

Workers Ahead

The next several chapters of Job detail the conversations between Job and his companions about the source of his woes. His friends told him that he must have sinned, or that his children must have sinned.

They told him that he was being punished. But time and again Job cried out, trying to understand what sin he had committed. Why was he being punished? He had covered himself with sackcloth and ashes and mourned before God in repentance, yet his situation continued to worsen.

We know from the beginning of Job's story that these calamities were not in response to sins Job or his family had committed. We know that there was nothing he could have done to change the outcome. These things happened for one reason only—so that God might be glorified. That sounds like a terrible reason for enduring suffering and pain to me. Why couldn't God have proven worthy of glory by blessing everyone beyond belief instead?

Job didn't understand the reason for his suffering and spent most of his time trying to determine its cause. He wanted to know what the charges were against him so that he could refute them or admit to them. But even in the midst of his suffering, he found a way to praise God.

Read Job 19:25.

For I know that my Redeemer lives,
*   and that at the last he will stand upon the earth;*

Even in the midst of his suffering, Job recalled that God still lived. He affirmed that God would redeem God's people. Job, who seems to have predated even Abraham, acknowledged God's presence on the earth and God's will to save. To admit this in the middle of such suffering was a huge act of faith. These few words show that Job had placed his trust in God and would not turn away from God—no matter what.

Job could feel God's presence and cried out to the one he trusted to listen, the one he hoped would answer. Even though his friends told him to stop and his wife told him to give up, Job persisted in seeking God's answer.

And an answer did come. God called out to Job from a whirlwind in chapter 38, asking just who Job thought he was. While Job had been carrying on, God had been about God's work in the world. Job learned that God's ways are not our ways, and Job was reminded that God has complete dominion.

God answered Job's prayer by reminding Job of God's place and of Job's place. When we place God in the rightful spot in our lives, we cannot help but be convicted of our shortcomings. Job responds in repentance.

Read Job 42:1-6.

Then Job answered the LORD:
² "I know that you can do all things,
*   and that no purpose of yours can be thwarted.*
³ 'Who is this that hides counsel without knowledge?'
Therefore I have uttered what I did not understand,
*   things too wonderful for me, which I did not know.*

How do you view the reason for Job's suffering? What does it teach you about God? about human nature?

What has caused you to questioned God? How did this time affect your ability to praise God?

How would living your life through the lens of this verse affect your prayers? your attitude? your actions?

What enables you to trust God even when others doubt?

When have you started to think too highly of yourself? How has God reminded you of your place in God's world?

While it is good to admit our hurts, angers, and frustrations to God, how might it go too far? How do we keep from falling into the "poor me" arrogance of Job?

⁴ 'Hear, and I will speak;
    I will question you, and you declare to me.'
⁵ I had heard of you by the hearing of the ear,
    but now my eye sees you;
⁶ therefore I despise myself,
    and repent in dust and ashes."

Job was convicted by his encounter with the living God. He realized that he was not God and, more importantly, that God did not answer to him. Job had put God on trial as he became more and more convinced of his own righteousness. God was not content to leave Job in that spot, but wanted him to realize his role in God's world. Who was Job to question God?

In the Rear View

At the end of Job's story, God did indeed come to Job and answer his requests. God also did something that only God can do; God offered Job grace.

Even though Job was a bit more than borderline offensive in his quest for justice, God relented. God did not continue to seek restitution from Job. God instead offered Job back all that had been taken from him. Job was given more wealth, more children, and more status than he had had before. God offered restoration and mercy.

God responds in the same manner to us. While we are certainly much lower than God, God sees fit to offer us relationship and restoration. God's grace reaches down to include even the least of us in God's kingdom.

And as the church, God offers us the challenge to share that same blessing and mercy with others. Grace is never something to keep for ourselves, but a gift to be given as a blessing.

Travel Log

Day 1:

Read again the second stanza of "Open My Eyes, That I May See" from the beginning of this lesson. What voice of truth does God have for you today? What falsehoods need to drift away? Where would God have you share this truth with others? Journal your responses below.

Day 2:

When have you lamented before God? When have you spoken honestly what was in your heart, even if it seemed presumptuous? How did it affect your relationship with God? What did you learn from the experience?

Make some notes below about some things that are in your heart now. You might want to write a prayer about them.

Day 3:

Think about the moments in your life when you have been the recipient of God's grace. How did you respond? What changes did you make? How did you pass that grace onto others?

List people to whom you need to extend grace. Add to the list ways in which you will do so.

Day 4:

Job's friends didn't believe him when he insisted that he had not sinned against God. They tried to get him to turn his back on God. When have friends been less than supportive of you? How did you deal with the situation? When have you failed to support others during their struggles? Write a few words to express forgiveness for their failure and to ask for forgiveness for your own failure.

Day 5:

Spend time today in prayer praising God. Praise God as creator, redeemer, and sustainer. Praise God for simple things like waking up and complex things like relationships. Do not complain! Take this opportunity to glorify God. Jot down some words of praise.

Day 6:

What was it like to pray yesterday without request or complaint? What did you learn about God? What did you learn about yourself? What can you share with your faith community about this experience? Record your responses to the questions in the space below.

Day 7:

Sometimes evaluating ourselves is a good thing. Look back over your prayer time for the past two weeks. What is working well? What might you need to change? Make adjustments as needed. How is God making God's will known to you today? Remember, prayer is a process that brings us into relationship with God. It is not a magic formula guaranteed to get results.

Create a list of people and situations for which you want to pray. Refer back to the list regularly, making notes about the progress of each one.

What to Do When Worship Stinks

Scripture for lesson: Isaiah 1:11-17

Let us open this lesson on prayer with the third verse from the hymn "Open My Eyes, That I May See" written by Clara H. Scott in 1895.

Open my mind that I may read,
More of Thy love in word and deed;
What shall I fear when Thou dost lead?
Only for light from Thee I plead.
Chorus
Silently now I wait for Thee,
Ready my God, Thy will to see,
Open my mind, illumine me,
Spirit divine!

Prep for the Journey

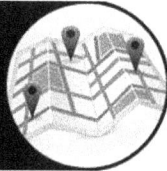

When a new minister comes to a church, one of the first requests usually made of her or him is to visit those members who have stopped attending for one reason or another. Honestly, these are some of my least favorite visits to make because I rarely feel prepared for or knowledgeable about their reasons for no longer attending. During one such visit, I asked a woman why she had stopped attending services. She looked up at me and said "I just didn't get anything out of them." When pressed for more detail, she said that she didn't feel fed, didn't like the music, and the children were too loud. I thanked her for her honesty, told her that those things were unlikely to be changed by the church, and wished her well in her search for a new congregation.

What reasons have others given you for not attending worship services regularly? What reasons do you give for missing church or other organized worship opportunities?

On the Road

How do you view worship? What things do you look for in a service? What things turn you away from a service?

What makes worship genuine to you? What about your church's worship practices might anger God?

When I told my elders how I had responded to this woman, they thought I was joking. Everyone wants the pews filled, no matter what it takes to get them that way. What I had done would certainly keep that from happening! But when we sat down and talked about it, they understood my reasoning. This woman's attitude about worship…well, it stunk. She did not feel catered to by the services. They did not make her feel good all of the time, they were not set to her schedule, nor did they meet her standards. She was missing the point.

Too often we all miss the point of worship. Worship is not about us. It is a time to glorify God, to please God, to offer ourselves up for God's use. When we turn the focus from God to us, then we begin to have problems that are as old as those of the Israelites!

Isaiah was a prophet during a very turbulent time in Israel's history. Political corruption, social injustices, and a host of other things were evidence of the people's moral decay. However, they thought they were remaining faithful to God because they continued to observe the feast days and offer sacrifices. God said they lacked the genuineness of real worship.

In the words from Isaiah we hear God speaking through the prophet to the people about worship and what worship had become. There was no escaping the fact that their worship angered God. But how could something intended to bring people closer to God anger God?

Read Isaiah 1:11-14.
What to me is the multitude of your sacrifices?
*   says the LORD;*
I have had enough of burnt offerings of rams
*   and the fat of fed beasts;*
I do not delight in the blood of bulls
*   or of lambs, or of goats.*

12 When you come to appear before me,
*   who asked this from your hand?*
*   Trample my courts no more;*
13 bringing offerings is futile;
*   incense is an abomination to me.*
New moon and sabbath and calling of convocation—
*   I cannot endure solemn assemblies with iniquity.*
14 Your new moons and your appointed festivals
*   my soul hates;*
they have become a burden to me,
*   I am weary of bearing them.*

24

Wow, God! Tell us how you really feel! These words sting, don't they? Most Christians believe that worship is part of living faithfully. There is value in attending worship even if all we do is just that—attend. But God seems to be saying here that worship for worship's sake is pointless. Going through the motions is not only unnecessary, but offensive!

Through Isaiah God told the people that their solemn assemblies, their festivals, and their offerings were a burden. There was nothing in their actions that brought joy to God anymore. If Isaiah were speaking to modern readers, perhaps this would come closer to his message from God: "Stop bringing gifts to me when you are ignoring the needs of others. Your children's Christmas program, your Sunday school, and your vacation Bible school offend me because they are not about me. You are busy with so many things, and I can't stand them; they keep you from doing what you should do."

The worship of the people had become overshadowed by ritual and by legalistic demands. There was an entire system devoted to making sure that people kept the rules and regulations of worship. These rules and regulations might have started out as ways to assure that God was pleased, but they became avenues that led to injustice and kept people from participating in the life of the family of God.

While we tend to think of these types of worship experiences as belonging to another time and space, some such rules are in place within congregations even now. In some churches people would be shunned if they did not dress up for a worship service. Simple choices such as the language used in a service reflects who would be welcome to attend. Some churches expect children to be loud and move, others expect them to be silent or to go to a special children's service. Even things such as a potluck can be overwhelming. Is there food for those with special dietary needs, such as vegetarians or diabetic individuals?

Scenic Route

The prophet was certainly harsh with the children of Israel—and with us. In fact, Isaiah went on to say that God was not only offended by what was being done, God actually refused to participate in or listen to the prayers of the people.

Read Isaiah 1:15-16.
When you stretch out your hands,
*   I will hide my eyes from you;*
even though you make many prayers,
*   I will not listen;*
*   your hands are full of blood.*

How would your faith community react to these words? How do you react?

What written and unwritten rules does your congregation have for worship? What are the reasons behind these rules? How do these rules allow people to worship God? How might they keep people from fully worshiping God?

How does it make you feel to know that God refused to listen to the people's prayers or be present when they worshiped?

25

¹⁶ Wash yourselves; make yourselves clean;
*   remove the evil of your doings*
*   from before my eyes;*
cease to do evil,

Isaiah warned the people that God would not hear the prayers of those who had blood on their hands. Since we no longer have sacrificial worship rituals, we should be okay, right? Wrong. Isaiah was speaking about a disconnect between what goes on in worship and what happens outside of worship. There was a difference between the people's worship and their actions. Can the same be said for us?

It is not enough to pray for peace and justice and then walk out the doors and ignore those very things on the way home. It is not enough to ask God to care for those in need when we refuse to share what we have with others. God is tired of our actions not matching our prayers. God is frustrated by the lack of real change in our hearts.

I once saw a poster in a homeless shelter that read "How can you worship a homeless man on Sunday and ignore one on Monday?" If what we do in worship, what we see in worship, what we say in worship does not affect our lives outside of worship, then it is pointless.

Workers Ahead — CAUTION

This passage can be very discouraging, especially in a study about prayer. At times we treat prayer and worship like an appointment, a commitment that has to be met even if we are not feeling up to it. Or perhaps we see them as ways to punch a card and get bonus points. "Come to church three times and take the next one off without penalty!" This way of viewing prayer and worship is oppressive. These words from scripture call us out on our falsehood and remind us why we are called to worship in the first place.

Read Isaiah 1:17.
*   ¹⁷learn to do good;*
seek justice,
*   rescue the oppressed,*
defend the orphan,
*   plead for the widow.*

What a simple, yet complicated calling! As God's people, we should be actively caring for those for whom God cares: the widow, the orphan, the oppressed, those in need of justice. Such actions must be a part of our lives and a part of our prayers. We cannot separate them. As James 1:27 says "Religion that is pure and undefiled before God, the Father, is this: to care for orphans and widows in their distress, and to keep oneself unstained by the world."

About what things might you pray on Sunday but ignore the rest of the week? Of what areas do you need to become more aware in your daily life instead of just your prayer or worship life?

When we gather for prayer and worship, what sort of things should we be doing? How can we have a prayer life and worship life that is pleasing to God?

Mrs. Margie was a children's Sunday school teacher at my home church. She spent every Sunday morning leading us in songs and worship time before we were dismissed to our individual Sunday school classes. She was a wonderful woman whom we all admired. What made Mrs. Margie so special was that she didn't just tell us she loved us; she showed us.

When we were having a hard time, Mrs. Margie made a point of encouraging us. She remembered our birthdays and celebrated them with us. Mrs. Margie prayed for each of us and sent us postcards letting us know that she was doing so. Mrs. Margie changed the world for me and many other children because she lived her life as she asked us to live ours.

There are many ways in which we can help those who are in need, so many ways to give feet to our prayers. Consider some of the following ministries that are ongoing because of The Cumberland Presbyterian Church or some of its individual congregations.

The Cumberland Presbyterian Children's Home in Denton, Texas, cares for children whose parents are unable to care for them, and offers a safe place for single-parent families to stay while they get back on their feet. The Children's Home provides housing, counseling, medical care, and lots of love.

The Stott-Wallace Offering provides funding for our missionaries who are serving in Asia, Africa, Central America, and South America. Some of these people are serving in countries that are closed to the gospel.

Sacred Sparks was organized by street pastor Lisa Cook in response to her calling to minister to people who are homeless in Nashville, Tennessee. In addition to ministering to these people spiritually, Lisa is their advocate. She helps them navigate bureaucracy, get medical care, find housing, and have access to clothing. Sometimes Lisa brings food and other needed items. Nashville Presbytery and the Brenthaven Cumberland Presbyterian Church, as well as other churches throughout the denomination, are strong supporters of this ministry.

Taste of Heaven is a food ministry hosted by the Sturgis Cumberland Presbyterian Church in Sturgis, Kentucky. Every Thursday night the church hosts a free meal, feeding 60-70 people every week. Many of those who come are school children, but the church also delivers meals to people who used to come but are no longer able to leave their homes easily. Members of the congregation participate by cooking, driving the church van to pick up people, and one farmer even donates a steer every year! Although this ministry provides food for the hungry, they build relationships by encouraging people to sit and talk as they eat. Taste of Heaven was never intended as a way to grow the congregation, but is simply one way of meeting the needs of people who are hungry in this economically depressed area.

Room in the Inn is an ecumenical ministry that offers shelter and compassion to people who are experiencing homelessness. Local congregations open their doors in order to welcome guests during the coldest months of the year—November through March. Cumberland

What examples do you have of living out your prayers and worship? How are you an example for others to follow? What might you need to change?

Presbyterians and their congregations are involved in this ministry in various locations. In fact, Rev. Lisa Anderson was instrumental in establishing the program in Memphis, Tennessee.

The Chinese Church in San Francisco, California, has an annual mission trip during which they minister to their Cumberland Presbyterian brothers and sisters in Choctaw Presbytery. They lead vacation Bible school, do maintenance work at Camp Israel Folsom or some of the churches, and fellowship with other Cumberland Presbyterians.

Research the ministries in your area in which you can participate as a faith community. You will find many more options than you think possible.

In the Rear View

The point of our prayers and worship is to glorify God, but how can we glorify God when our actions don't reflect our worship and prayers? The Christian church has faced this question throughout its existence; the question is becoming increasingly more pronounced today.

As a group, take time to brainstorm ways you can go about putting feet to your prayers. Don't be afraid to suggest something; all ideas are worth exploring. As a group, covenant to pray about these opportunities. Ask God to show you where God wants you to join existing work or where you are needed to begin a new ministry.

You don't have to re-invent service. You just need to be willing to follow where God leads. Allow time for everyone to record the brainstormed ideas by writing them down, taking a picture of the list, or even sending out an email that includes the list to other members.

If your faith community is engaged in a ministry that gives feet to your prayers, let us know so that we can share it with others! Send your ministry opportunities to Cindy Martin at chm@cumberland.org.

Travel Log

Day 1:

Read again the third stanza of "Open My Eyes, That I May see" from the beginning of this lesson. What part of your mind is closed to God's word? How does this scripture show you God's love in word and deed? How are you letting God lead? Make some notes below as you reflect on these questions.

Day 2:

Take out the list of ministry opportunities generated by your group. What appeals to you about them? What scares you? Write a few words or sentences about how each one would help you live out your prayers in day-to-day living.

Day 3:

When you think about people whose actions and prayer life seem to match, who comes to mind? What things especially stand out? How can you exemplify such behavior for others?

Write a note to one or more of the people you identified, telling them how important their example has been for you.

Day 4:

This passage from Isaiah is challenging, to say the least. Re-read these words and make note of things that you see differently today then you did the first time you looked at them. What has become clearer? Where do you still need guidance?

Day 5:

Put feet to your prayers today. Do something to help someone, or address a situation about which you have been praying. Journal about your thoughts and feelings as you approach the situation and then reflect on them afterward.

Day 6:

Of what have you become more aware during the past several days? Are their suddenly needy kids everywhere you turn? Are the needs of people who are homeless on your heart? Or are people who are unable to leave their homes coming to mind more frequently?

Write down any such observations and insights. Pray about your list. Take a cue from your increased awareness and seek ways to engage more with meeting these needs.

Day 7:

Isaiah's vision called for action of the people. In 2:4, Isaiah said:

He shall judge between the nations,
    and shall arbitrate for many peoples;
they shall beat their swords into plowshares,
    and their spears into pruning hooks;
nation shall not lift up sword against nation,
    neither shall they learn war any more.

What role could prayer and worship have in leading to the culmination of this prophecy? What role do we, as the church, have in seeking a world of God's justice and peace? Record some of your responses to these questions.

Words to Live By

Scripture for lesson: Matthew 6:5-13

L
FAITH
F
E

Let us open this lesson on prayer with the third verse from the hymn "Open My Eyes, That I May See" written by Clara H. Scott in 1895.

Open my mouth, and let me bear
Gladly the warm truth everywhere;
Open my heart, and let me prepare
Love with Thy children thus to share.
Chorus
Silently now I wait for Thee,
Ready, my God, Thy will to see;
Open my heart, illumine me,
Spirit divine!

Prayer is a deeply personal thing. It may also be a very public act. As a minister, I find myself being asked to pray more than I would like. Every time we bless a meal people look to me to say the words. When I am in a Bible study, people expect me to pray.

The other day I went to my son's daycare and was greeted at the door by a group of workers. They were gathering to pray for someone's niece. There stood 20 women in a circle, but not one of them felt able to lead the others in prayer. They were so relieved when the preacher stepped through the door. I was glad to pray with them, but I wonder what might have happened had I not come. Would anyone have stepped forward to help these women voice their concerns to God?

Prep for the Journey

When I was a teenager, my youth group did a skit for our church. It was based on the Lord's Prayer. One person began praying the Lord's Prayer and was interrupted by the voice of God. God and this

When have you struggled to find the words to pray? How do you handle being asked to pray in public? How often do you pray in private?

Watch this clip on YouTube to see a version of the Lord's Prayer skit: https://www.youtube.com/watch?v=4BleD6-C0XU

person went back and forth and back and forth over the words of this prayer. What do they mean? What do you mean when you say them? It changed my perspective on prayer in general and on this prayer in particular.

Prayer has been a topic of discussion throughout the history of Christianity. But very few people tend to agree on how best to pray. There are those who say that when praying you should only use words found in the scriptures. There are those who bow their heads, close their eyes, and pray silently. There are those who pray while doing things like walking or jogging. I would dare to say there are as many different ways to pray as there are people praying. So, how do we address the "proper" way to pray as Christians today?

On the Road

In Matthew 6:9-13 we find a guideline for prayer that Jesus gave to his followers. This guideline has become one of the most recognized and prayed prayers of all time. But what does it mean, and how should we use it? In order to answer those questions, we need to take a small look back at what comes before this prayer in scripture.

Read Matthew 6:5-6.

"And whenever you pray, do not be like the hypocrites; for they love to stand and pray in the synagogues and at the street corners, so that they may be seen by others. Truly I tell you, they have received their reward. 6 But whenever you pray, go into your room and shut the door and pray to your Father who is in secret; and your Father who sees in secret will reward you."

Jesus was teaching the multitudes in what has come to be known as the Sermon on the Mount. A good deal of those teachings involve looking at the way things have been done and changing them to reflect God's love.

This particular passage on prayer begins with Christ telling his followers to pray in a manner very different from that to which they were accustomed. The religious elite of the day had taken to saying their prayers in very public places. They thanked God for their blessings, their goodness, and their righteousness—often openly comparing themselves to others.

Prayer is never for the sake of comparison or building one's self up in front of others. Jesus told his followers to pray in secret, giving their concerns and joys to God personally, one-on-one. God, who is present in all places, will hear you if you pray in the streets or if you pray in your closet. Long, loud prayers were a way to elevate one's status with the religious elite, but not with God.

What rules or guidelines have you heard about prayer? Which do you personally follow?

How do you feel about Jesus calling people hypocrites because of the way they were praying? Have you ever felt hypocritical when praying? If so, why?

Jesus went on to say that using an impressive vocabulary or the "right words" is not a pleasing way to offer prayers. God, the true and authentic God, was not impressed by babbling or long-windedness.

Read Matthew 6:7-8.

"When you are praying, do not heap up empty phrases as the Gentiles do; for they think that they will be heard because of their many words. ⁸ Do not be like them, for your Father knows what you need before you ask him."

God will not be tricked into hearing or answering our prayers. No amount of flattery will convince God to be on our side. The Gentiles used a lot of words and phrases to entreat their gods to listen to them. But the Creator knows our needs and concerns and will not be moved by flowery language.

Scenic Route

After giving instruction on what not to do, Jesus finally offered words to guide his followers in prayer. While we often repeat these words as a prayer in and of themselves, they are much more than that. These words are not just something to be memorized. They are a template of a way to pray that gets at the heart of what we need to do—develop a relationship with God and recognize that God already has a relationship with us.

Read Matthew 6:9-13.
"Pray then in this way:
Our Father in heaven,
    hallowed be your name.
    ¹⁰ Your kingdom come.
Your will be done,
        on earth as it is in heaven.
    ¹¹Give us this day our daily bread.
    ¹²And forgive us our debts,
        as we also have forgiven our debtors.
    ¹³ And do not bring us to the time of trial,
        but rescue us from the evil one."

Jesus taught that we should begin our prayers by acknowledging who God is and what God's place is in the world. God is to be hallowed, revered, and worshiped. God is ruler over heaven and earth, and we should offer praise and respect. By acknowledging these things about God, we also admit that we are not holy or ruler over all heaven and earth. We must begin with a focus on God.

How do you feel when someone seems to pray forever? when he or she uses "biblical" language rather than conversational words?

When you pray the Lord's Prayer, how much do you consider the words you are praying? How can you improve your focus on these familiar words?

How do you normally begin your prayers? How does that reflect your view of God and God's identity?

In what ways are you participating in God's kingdom on earth? How are you living out God's call to "do justice, and to love kindness, and to walk humbly with your God"? (Micah 6:8)

How often do you trust God for your daily bread? How easy is it to trust God to provide? Of what does your daily bread, your essential needs, consist?

How do you understand forgiveness? How easy is it for you to offer forgiveness? accept forgiveness?

What debts do you have that need to be forgiven? How can you forgive others? In what ways do you see forgiveness as a type of release?

Once God has been recognized and praised, the prayer continues by asking that God's kingdom come and God's will be done. These words remind us that we should be seeking to bring about the kingdom of God here on earth. Jesus frequently said that the "kingdom of God is at hand." The kingdom is not something on which we wait, but something in which we participate.

The next portion of the prayer is where so many of us get hung up. Jesus told us to ask for our daily bread. We are to ask God for the essentials in life, but far too often we get caught up in asking for everything, including the kitchen sink, each time we pray. This portion of Jesus' instruction reminds us of the days the Israelites lived in the wilderness. Every morning for forty years (except the Sabbath), God provided daily bread, or manna, for God's people. While they were unsure of what to call it, they were thankful for it and took enough for each day. If they took more than they needed for one day (except the day before the Sabbath), it would spoil. God provides what we need for each day.

Workers Ahead — CAUTION

Forgiveness is the next topic of the prayer. We are to ask God for forgiveness. Sounds pretty good, right? We all have fallen short of the glory of God! Forgiveness is something that helps renew our relationship with God. To be forgiven is to be offered the gift of full relationship once more. We are no longer tethered to our sins and are free to embrace God fully. It's perhaps my favorite part of this prayer.

However, it is closely followed by the hardest part of prayer to me—forgiving others. We ask God to forgive our debts, as we forgive our debtors. Does this mean that God doesn't forgive us unless we forgive everyone else first? I don't believe so. I think it points to the reality that until we forgive others we cannot understand what forgiveness really means.

The Lord's Prayer recognizes one painful truth. We are all in debt. Think about that for a moment. Each of us is in debt to God and to others. Farmers often use operating loans to plant their crops. We have mortgages on our homes. Students get loans to pay for their education.

Not only are we in financial debt, but we are spiritually in debt as well. While we were yet sinners Christ died for us, says Romans. This debt is one that we cannot repay. It is a gift, a celebration, an opportunity for new life. When we recognize this forgiveness of debts as the gift of release that it is, we are offered the opportunity also to release others from their debts. When we forgive, we are refocusing our attention away from ourselves and onto ways that we can help others.

The final part of this model of prayer asks to be kept from the time of trial and to be rescued from evil. If we are actively seeking out the will of God on earth, we will encounter trials and evil. Living according to Jesus' teachings is not a promise of an easy and carefree life. After all, Jesus was killed because of his teachings.

We are to pray that God will keep us from trials and evils that might sway us to abandon every belief we have professed. We ask God to help us continue on this difficult path we have chosen to walk. We put ourselves in God's hands as we try to be kingdom people.

In the Rear View

The Lord's Prayer is not simply a passage to quote once or twice a week. It is a model of what faithful prayer from faithful people should be. Living by the words of the Lord's Prayer is a challenging ideal, one that will take effort, but one that could change us and the world in which we live.

As a group, gather together and pray the Lord's Prayer. Allow time between the phrases for meditation upon their meaning. You may want to pray on one phrase a day throughout the week so that you can let the meanings become clearer to you.

When might it be hard to follow the kingdom way? What might God's protection look like? How can we help one another not to fall victim to trials and evil?

How can you begin living the Lord's Prayer today? What might living the Lord's Prayer look like in a community of faith?

37

Travel Log

Day 1:

Read again the fourth stanza of "Open My Eyes, That I May see" from the beginning of this lesson. What part of your heart is closed to God's word? In what ways do you need to further open your heart to allow God's love to dwell within? Journal some of your thoughts about these questions.

Day 2:

Too often the words in Matthew 6:5-6 are used to deter people from praying out loud in a group or in public worship. How do these verses relate to public worship? How can the church encourage public and private prayer? Make note of some suggestions you would like to share with those who have responsibility for planning worship in your congregation.

Day 3:

When you think of the kingdom of God, what comes to mind? What would change if the kingdom was on earth as it is in heaven? Write a few words or sentences as to how you would describe this idea to someone else.

Day 4:

Daily bread is an important thing. There are many people who do not receive daily bread in our world. What can be done to help this? How can you help someone else get their daily bread? List the agencies in your community that provide food to people who are hungry. Determine some ways that you and your faith community can be supportive of those efforts.

Day 5:

   Forgiveness is one of the hardest and yet most wonderful things to do. Whom do you need to forgive? What is keeping you from doing so? Write a prayer in which you ask God to begin opening you up to forgiveness and to show you ways to begin the process.

Day 6:

   How have you been lead into temptation or times of trial? How did you handle it? How was God present in that situation? Record some of your reflections on these questions.

Day 7:

Matthew's version of the Lord's Prayer acknowledges that the world is not what it should be. What is not as it should be in your world? Where do you need to let God in to redeem and restore? In what areas do you need to seek God's will more intentionally? Make some notes about these areas. Reflect back on them during the next few weeks as you continue to pray for God's guidance.

Bootstrap Religion

Scripture for lesson: Luke 18:9-14

Let's open this lesson on prayer with this verse from the hymn "Sweet Hour of Prayer" written by William W. Walford in 1845.

Sweet hour of prayer, sweet hour of prayer!
The joys I feel, the bliss I share,
Of those whose anxious spirits burn
With strong desires for thy return!
With such I hasten to the place
Where God my Savior shows His face,
And gladly take my station there,
And wait for thee, sweet hour of prayer!

Prep for the Journey

My grandmother always had a special place at the dinner table. She sat at what she called the "foot" of the table, across the length of her large dining table from my grandfather, who sat at the "head." For years I was convinced that my grandmother was as dyslexic as me, because she was obviously the center of every family meal. She was the one who brought in the beautifully prepared food. She was the one on whom we waited before praying and beginning to eat. She was the one to whom we turned most often during the meal for seconds, for dessert, for approval. That made her important, and important people sit at the "head" of the table. I learned later that she sat at the "foot" so that she could serve us. While she took the position of servant, I had seen her more as a queen holding court.

How would you treat a servant? How would you treat an honored guest? If there are differences, explain why.

On the Road

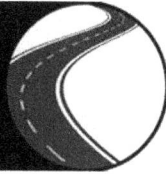

The lesson for today is a parable, although we don't often treat it as such. A parable is a story that uses everyday examples to make a point. Some parables have a twist that make them more memorable. The closest things we have to parables in modern writing are fables. These stories immerse the reader or listener in a parallel universe and give them a new perspective on the world in which they live. Jesus used parables as a way of making a point to his listeners.

This parable has two participants: a Pharisee and a tax collector. Even in our time, most people will quickly view the tax collector as evil and the Pharisee as good, possibly without knowing what a Pharisee was!

Read Luke 18:9-10.

He also told this parable to some who trusted in themselves that they were righteous and regarded others with contempt: [10] *"Two men went up to the temple to pray, one a Pharisee and the other a tax collector.*

Verse 9 tells us that this story is about people who trust in themselves and view others with contempt. It is rare that we get such a description before hearing the story.

The Pharisees were popular with the general public. As middle-class citizens, many people trusted the Pharisees over the elitist Sadducees. The Pharisees interpreted the Law of Moses and applied it to current situations. They were partly responsible for all of the nuances that made the Law so burdensome. However, their absolute respect of and adherence to the Law garnered the respect of common people, who tried to emulate them. They held a certain level of status in the community and had tremendous influence over the people. The Pharisee in this parable had gone to the Temple to pray.

At the same time the Pharisee was arriving at the Temple, a tax collector also entered the gates. Tax collectors were more dreaded than any IRS agent today. Often pressed into service by the Roman government, it was their job to collect the taxes imposed by the Romans. However, there were no provisions to protect people from paying more than their fair share of tax. Whatever extra amounts were collected usually lined the tax collector's pocket. Tax collectors quickly gained a reputation of being unscrupulous at best, downright thieves at worst.

Because of their association with the Romans, who were Gentiles, tax collectors were considered to be unclean. Just imagine such a person stepping onto the grounds of the most holy site for the Jewish culture. People would have avoided him like the plague!

What assumptions have you made about people based on their background or career? How accurate are these assumptions? When has someone judged you positively or negatively simply by knowing your religion or occupation?

What group of people in our society has a lot of influence over the general populace? Why? In what way is this influence healthy or unhealthy?

What groups of people do you avoid? How would those people be treated if they entered your church?

How can you express thanks without being like the Pharisee?

Who are the tax collectors in your midst? How can you be more accepting of them?

Why would the Pharisee not have been justified? Why was the tax collector held in higher regard? How are your prayers sometimes like the Pharisee's? the tax collector's?

Read Luke 22:11-12.

The Pharisee, standing by himself, was praying thus, 'God, I thank you that I am not like other people: thieves, rogues, adulterers, or even like this tax collector. 12 I fast twice a week; I give a tenth of all my income.'

The Pharisee stood up and spoke words with which others in the Temple surely agreed. How wonderful of him to thank God for the blessings in his life. How holy of him to be that dedicated to fasting and tithing. He sounds like the perfect church member! Sign him up to lead the stewardship campaign or head the Building and Grounds committee. For those of us looking at him from the outside, it sounds as though he had his act together.

You can almost see the crowd smiling and approving, nodding their heads in agreement. Then the focus shifts from the Pharisee in the middle of the picture to the man over to the side.

Read Luke 22:13.

But the tax collector, standing far off, would not even look up to heaven, but was beating his breast and saying, 'God, be merciful to me, a sinner!'

While the Pharisee was standing in the limelight, the tax collector lurked in the shadows. He stood away from the crowd, not trying to impress anyone. He didn't even dare to look up to the heavens. Instead he stood there pounding his chest and crying out, "God, be merciful to me! I know I am a sinner!" How disgraceful! Who would do that in the Temple? Who would want an admitted sinner in their midst? Didn't he have any shame?

The crowd in the story, and probably the ones listening, were made uncomfortable by this man and his outburst. That's just not how things were done in those days. It isn't really how things are done in our day, either. Surely Jesus would point to the Pharisee as an example of proper prayer.

Read Luke 22:14.

I tell you, this man went down to his home justified rather than the other; for all who exalt themselves will be humbled, but all who humble themselves will be exalted."

There it is—the twist! The tax collector, despised and maligned by society, returned home justified. The Pharisee went back home still carrying his sin. This ending was not what the crowds expected, but God often turns things upside down.

Scenic Route

While the Pharisee might have appeared more righteous and more holy, the tax collector returned home justified, forgiven, redeemed. On the surface it didn't make a whole lot of sense to those who heard the story, nor does it to us. But when you look at the content of the two men's prayers, it becomes clear.

The Pharisee thanked God, but he thanked God that he was not like those people. He was grateful to be better than the common rabble—better than the thieves, the unlawful, those who were sexually immoral, and even the tax collector. He boasted about his religious actions. He followed the rules and kept his toes on the right side of the line. Notice the common thread running through his prayer?

Time and again the Pharisee said "I" as in "I have done" or "I am not." Everything in his prayer was about him. It was all about what he had done. The Pharisee had become a victim of what I like to call "bootstrap religion." He was proud of his self-reliance, of his contained behavior. The Pharisee was thankful that God had given him the ability to make something of himself and he wanted the world to know that he had done just that!

The tax collector, on the other hand, had no doubt about his place and about God's place. While the Pharisee was patting himself on the back, the tax collector couldn't even bring himself to look up toward heaven. He beat his breast, mourning before God because of his sins. Unlike the Pharisee, the tax collector knew he was a sinner in need of redemption.

By acknowledging his place and God's place, the tax collector allowed God to do the work of justification in him. Voicing his weakness and his need to God gave him the opportunity to receive the mercy for which he had begged.

Workers Ahead

Justification comes through God reaching out in mercy to helpless sinners. This concept is one with which we can struggle for a lifetime. We don't want to admit that we can't do it all on our own. We don't want to seek help from God or anyone else. But when we refuse to recognize our sin, when we fail to see our need, we cannot accept God's forgiveness.

When have you fallen into the "bootstrap religion" trap? What is the error in this kind of thinking?

When was the last time you were brutally honest before God about your sin and your need for mercy? When was the last time you were honest with yourself about these things?

Why do you think it is so difficult to admit that we can't do it all on our own?

Why is it important to confess our sins? Why should it matter to us? Why does it matter to God?

How does your faith community handle confession of sin? What are some potential benefits of having it be a normal part of worship? What are some drawbacks?

My children struggle with the idea of forgiveness. When Mom or Dad gets angry, my 11-year-old's first response is, "I'm sorry," (usually screamed at the top of her lungs). When we ask what she is sorry for, there is rarely an answer. Sometimes her response is, "I'm sorry you got mad" or "I'm sorry that I got caught." Those answers do not acknowledge that she did anything wrong. They are, at best, an attempt to pacify us until she can get what she wants.

Many congregations no longer offer a time during which the worshipers join together to confess their sins. In some churches, people claim that the prayer of confession only makes them feel guilty. I have also heard that it's something they only do during lent.

However, several months ago a young woman in my congregation said that the confession of sin was her favorite part of our worship service. When I asked why, she said, "I don't always think about my sin, why I need forgiveness. It reminds me that I need Jesus just as much, if not more, than the next guy."

In our society, it is sometimes hard to admit that we are dependent upon anyone for anything. As Christians, one of the first things we have to admit is our dependence upon God's grace.

In the Rear View

By confessing our sins to God, we allow space for God to enter into our lives anew. We also remind ourselves of God's rightful place in our lives. We are not saved by ourselves. As Ephesians 2:8 says "For by grace you have been saved through faith, and this is not your own doing; it is the gift of God."

"Bootstrap religion" gives us the illusion that we are in command, and that our works, our good deeds, our "holiness" will bring us into God's kingdom. However, it is just that—an illusion. God offers us grace through Jesus, which is the only way any of us can be saved.

As a class, take a moment and join in this confession of sin, or one from your community of faith's tradition.

Lord, in your mercy, hear our prayer. We come before you, most holy God, aware of your rightful place as Savior. We praise you with our lips and our hearts. As we stand in your presence, we are made aware of our shortcomings, our failings, our sin. By deeds of commission and omission, we have neglected those in need. With malice in our hearts, we have assassinated character. Without much thought, we have elevated ourselves above others. Lord, for these sins and others, we humbly repent. Forgive us, we pray. Purify us through Christ and make us justified before you. In the name of Jesus Christ we boldly pray. Amen.

Travel Log

Day 1:

Read again the stanza of "Sweet Hour of Prayer" from the beginning of this lesson. Where do you go to seek God's face? What bliss of God could you share today? Jot down your thoughts as you consider the questions.

Day 2:

Jesus often used parables to teach. Which parable is your favorite? Why does it resonate with you? If you don't have a favorite parable, which one is the most memorable? Why? Write down some things that make this parable your favorite.

Day 3:

Some of us learn better by doing. Rewrite a parable in modern language. You can change the characters and/or examples to ones that would be easily recognizable in modern society. Use this parable as the basis for your prayers today.

Day 4:

You have heard the saying "Confession is good for the soul." What do you think about this saying? How might you alter it to make it truer for you? What in particular about confession is good? Journal your responses to these questions.

Day 5:

Re-read your church's prayer of confession from this week. If you do not have one, re-read the prayer of confession from this week's lesson. What stands out to you? What phrase seems to hit home today? How does it feel different to you than when you first read it? What has changed? Write your own prayer of confession.

Day 6:

We confess our sins to God, seeking forgiveness and restoration of relationship. Look up the definitions for confession and apology. Write some key words about each in the space below. Which of these two are you more likely to do? Which might improve your relationship with God and others?

Day 7:

Sometimes we let where we pray dictate how we pray. During your prayer time today, move to a different location. If you are usually inside, go outside. If you are usually at your desk, go stand by a window. How did this change affect your prayers? What did you notice that you are not normally aware of? How was your experience different? How was it the same? Jot down some notes about what you liked or disliked about praying in a different location.

Isn't That Just Like a Woman?

Scripture for lesson: Luke 18:1-8

Let us open this lesson on prayer with another verse from the hymn "Sweet Hour of Prayer" written by William W. Walford in 1845.

Sweet hour of prayer! sweet hour of prayer!
Thy wings shall my petition bear
To Him whose truth and faithfulness
Engage the waiting soul to bless.
And since He bids me seek His face,
Believe His Word and trust His grace,
I'll cast on Him my every care,
And wait for thee, sweet hour of prayer!

Prep for the Journey

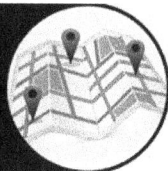

I have two cats, Milo (16) and Shadow (6). They are sweet, wonderful, happy kitties. They are good with the kids, they keep my feet warm at night, and help me calm down when I'm stressed. They are fantastic! But they have this one really annoying habit: They refuse to eat out of their bowl if they can see even a hint of the bottom of the bowl. They will hunt me down, meowing at amazingly loud levels, to get me to come to the bowl any time of day or night if the tiniest hint of blue is visible! After years of telling them they still had plenty of food, after much time spent spreading the food out to make it look full, after a lot of frustration, I learned something: Every night and every morning I put fresh food in the bowl, regardless of whether or not I think they need it. Some people, like my husband, might say that the cats have trained me to get what they want. I would say that I have stopped the annoying meowing epidemic!

What sorts of things annoy you? How do you handle being annoyed? What are you willing to do to stop an annoyance?

We begin with another parable from Luke chapter 18. In this story we have a widow and an unjust judge pitted against each other. It is a battle royal. Who will emerge victorious?

The first time this particular passage came up in seminary, someone whispered from the back row, "Isn't that just like a woman?" It got quite a few laughs and several smiles. The idea behind it was that if a woman nags long enough, someone will give in to her just to get her to be quiet. The back row response has always bothered me, but I've not known how to respond to it until working on this lesson.

Read Luke 18:1-3.

Then Jesus told them a parable about their need to pray always and not to lose heart. ² He said, "In a certain city there was a judge who neither feared God nor had respect for people. ³ In that city there was a widow who kept coming to him and saying, 'Grant me justice against my opponent.'

Jesus used many parables as he taught his disciples and other followers. Parables allowed him to make a point without singling out particular people or situations, which may have made the teaching easier for people to hear and accept. In the parable under consideration in this lesson, Jesus took his listeners into the world of an unjust judge and a widow.

Jesus described the judge as one who had no fear of God or respect for people. A judge who did not fear God placed his understanding of right and wrong, of truth and justice, into his own hands instead of relying on the Law of Moses. We don't really know much about the ways in which justice was administered in Jesus' day, especially in the villages. Apparently, rulings could be levied by a single person. If this person was corrupt and the one who was seeking justice could not afford to bribe the judge or did not have any power in the community, it was tough luck.

Women had little to no standing in the society of Jesus' day; widows were especially vulnerable. If they did not have an adult male child to care for them, they were often at the mercy of the community and the religious organizations. Usually any property or things of value that had belonged to their husbands was passed to a male relative or given to the synagogue, where it was doled out as needed. Unfortunately, widows were often left to fend for themselves.

This particular widow was seeking justice. She had been wronged, perhaps by family, perhaps by the religious system, perhaps by a crooked used tent dealer. Whatever the case, she went to the judge to seek his ruling.

How just are our judicial systems? In what ways might they need to be improved? What role might the church be able to have in working for any needed changes?

Who are the widows of our day and time? Who struggles to be heard in our courts of law? in courts of public opinion? What is the faith community's responsibility to these groups of people?

Jesus said that the widow continued to go before the Judge. I can imagine that it was difficult for her to continue to fight for her rights after being dismissed several times. Yet, she did not feel that she had received justice, and was determined to get a ruling against those who had harmed her. She refused to give up.

Read Luke 18:4-5.

"For a while he refused; but later he said to himself, 'Though I have no fear of God and no respect for anyone, ⁵ yet because this widow keeps bothering me, I will grant her justice, so that she may not wear me out by continually coming.'"

The judge was finally worn down by the widow's constant petitions. He gave her the justice she sought, but not because it was the right thing to do, and not even because it was the easiest thing to do. He did it because she had so thoroughly annoyed him that he could not take it anymore.

Scenic Route

What a strange story about prayer! If we stop with the scripture here, the message seems pretty clear: Bug God long enough and you will get what you want. If you continually whine and complain, God will grow tired of you and give you what you ask. This is the kind of story kids would love, because most of them know that a certain level of annoyance can get them things they want, especially when said annoyance happens in public. But this can't be the message Jesus wanted the disciples and us to take from this scripture, can it? Thankfully, the scripture does not end here.

Read Luke 18:6-8.

And the Lord said, "Listen to what the unjust judge says. ⁷ And will not God grant justice to his chosen ones who cry to him day and night? Will he delay long in helping them? ⁸ I tell you, he will quickly grant justice to them. And yet, when the Son of Man comes, will he find faith on earth?"

The unjust judge can't be God, whose very nature is just. However, we may sometimes wonder if God will grant justice. Many of us have prayed fervently for something that at the time seemed just, only to have God either delay responding or even say no. It would seem just for God to help a person find fulfilling employment after more than two years of being without a job. Justice would have seemed to be served by God healing a young father whose family, church, and community needed him.

When have you refused to give up, despite the odds? What enabled you to continue your quest? What was the end result?

How do you react to being badgered? When have you badgered someone else? Based on your experiences, how effective is badgering?

When have you given in because someone continued to annoy you? How did you feel about your decision?

How do you deal with situations like the ones mentioned in the text? Where do you find justice in those scenarios?

What have you learned by having to wait for God's response to your pleas? Did your prayers change as you waited? If so, why?

How do you respond to the thought of a persistent God? Why do you think God continues to seek you?

What is the difference between praying boldly and praying in other ways? How willing are you to pray boldly?

The widow sought the judge repeatedly. We don't know how long it was before the judge finally granted her request. Maybe we need to wait for justice so that we are better prepared for what it will mean in our lives. Maybe God is teaching us something. Maybe what we think is justice does not fit within God's plan. Only God has those answers!

God may actually be more like the widow than the judge. God is persistent. God never gives up on us—even when, time and time and time again, we fall short of the goal. God continues to offer us grace and forgiveness. God continues to seek relationship. God continues to love us even when we think we are unlovable.

We serve a persistent God, one who will not stop looking for the lost sheep. Because of God's persistence we, too, can be persistent. Does this mean we can beg and complain until we get what we want? No. We can be persistent in seeking God's justice. We can be persistent in asking that God's will be done. We can be persistent in crying out "Thy kingdom come!"

If an unjust judge is capable of doing right every once in a while, then certainly the God of justice can be counted on to provide justice for God's people. We must persist in asking. We must persist in praying for and acting toward justice. When we persist in asking, praying, and acting, we participate with God in kingdom work here and now.

Workers Ahead

People are not always willing to pray boldly. I have heard several church members and attendees pray for justice, for peace, and for healing. However, they almost always add on the tag line "but, thy will be done." God's will is justice, healing, and peace. These are spelled out multiple times in the scriptures. By praying for these things, we are seeking God's will. "Thy will be done" is a hugely important prayer, but when we tack it onto a prayer, we are just covering our bases in case what we want to have happen doesn't occur in our time frame.

I recently heard a story of a church that felt called to start serving people with special needs who live in their community. The only problem was that no one in the church had special needs or had any connections to the special needs community. They began praying that they could be a small part of helping with special needs and started by collecting an offering for the Special Olympics. It wasn't much, but it was a start. They continued to pray together, to learn more together. They persisted in finding those whom they could help.

Eventually they were put into contact with someone who ran a residency program for special needs adults in a neighboring town. This small church has become a partner with the home. They help with simple things like washer and dryer connection replacements and complicated things like job placement and training. This partnership didn't develop overnight. The church members were persistent in their prayers and in their seeking. They did not stop until God showed them a way to serve in the manner to which they had been called.

It has taken over fifteen years for this ministry to flourish, but it definitely has. The church is looking to open an additional residence for people who have special needs. They are also considering how to become advocates in the legal system for these blessed sons and daughters of God.

In the Rear View

We are so blessed that God is persistent in seeking us out. We are called to persist in seeking God's will in the world, in our churches, and in our lives. This parable points us toward an amazing miracle. Through our persistent prayer we are able to participate in God's miracles of healing, restoration, and justice. We are allowed the privilege of coming along beside God and helping to bring the present/not-yet kingdom of God into the world.

"Isn't that just like a woman?" we may hear people say. Perhaps we can turn the phrase around and say, "Isn't that just like a woman or man of faith? Never giving up, never giving in, until God's justice makes itself known!"

What is your dream ministry or area of ministry? Where do you feel called to bring justice? What is keeping you from participating in that calling?

Travel Log

Day 1:

Read again the stanza of "Sweet Hour of Prayer" from the beginning of this lesson. Where do you go to seek God's face? What bliss of God could you share today? What cares do you need to give God today? How can you find your rest in God? List those things that you will give to God today. Pray about them as you release yourself from the worry and stress.

Day 2:

Where do you feel a calling for justice? How can you persist in petitioning God for that justice? How can you enlist others to help you with this petition? As you think about situations in your community and beyond that are crying out for justice, make some notes as to where God may be calling you to serve.

Day 3:

One of the best things about keeping a prayer journal is looking back through it to find where God has answered prayers. How do you keep track of requests for prayer? Which ones have been answered recently? About which requests have you been the most persistent? How has God answered the prayer in a way different from what you prayed? Reflect about your prayers and record your thoughts and feelings.

Day 4:

Take a prayer list and place it where you will see it daily. Pray for the requests you see. Make notes of how God acts in those situations. Take the opportunity to lift up these prayers frequently.

Day 5:

Think of your journey of faith thus far. When has God pursued you? Where have you seen God's persistence in seeking you and bringing you close? How can these times be helpful to others? As you consider these questions, journal your thoughts.

Day 6:

Write a letter or poem to a friend or family member who is struggling to find God. Share with this person how God pursued you and pursues all of God's children. Pray over the writing and ask God if you should send the poem or letter, or in what other way you should express these things to your friend or family member.

Day 7:

    Prayer is a conversation with God, but all too frequently we do all of the talking and fail to pause to listen for God. Spend intentional time listening for and to God. What words of comfort or peace, challenge or hope does God have for you today? How would God have you share these words with another person? Jot down the words and thoughts God gives to you.

Eyes Wide Shut

Scripture for lesson: Luke 22:39-46

Let us open this lesson on prayer with this verse from the hymn "Sweet Hour of Prayer" written by William W. Walford in 1845.

> Sweet hour of prayer! sweet hour of prayer!
> That calls me from a world of care,
> And bids me at my Father's throne
> Make all my wants and wishes known.
> In seasons of distress and grief,
> My soul has often found relief,
> And oft escaped the tempter's snare,
> By thy return, sweet hour of prayer!

Prep for the Journey

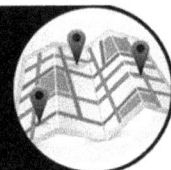

My three-year-old son has recently discovered prayer. He is not entirely sure how the whole thing works (much like most of us), but he knows it is important. Before we eat dinner he calls out, "Is it time to pray yet?" When he goes to bed, he grabs my neck and says, "Pray for me, Mommy." When I drop him off at school, he asks me to pray for him. I ask God to bless him with a good day and then he says, "Amen God, and Mommy's day too!" Just last night at a church Bible study we were getting ready to pray and he got into my lap and said "Mommy, you pray. Pray with your eyes shut. I pray with my eyes open so I know what's happening."

Praying with my eyes open was not something that my parents would have allowed as I was growing up. You prayed with your eyes closed so that you wouldn't be distracted by what was going on around you. But perhaps there is something to the words my three-year-old said. Perhaps praying with our eyes open to see what's happening is exactly what Jesus had in mind in today's scripture passage.

> What rituals do you have surrounding prayer? In what way did you learn how to pray and when to pray? When did you learn that prayer was different depending on who was praying?

Jesus and his disciples had gone to Jerusalem to celebrate the Passover. All Jewish males age 13 and older were expected to make the pilgrimage to Jerusalem for this holiest of feasts. Of course, with so many people coming into the city, lodging was at a premium. Many people, likely including Jesus and his friends, camped amidst the groves on the Mount of Olives during such festival times. The Garden of Gethsemane was in this same area.

The disciples and Jesus had shared the Passover meal, after which they headed back to where they were staying. Along the way, they stopped in the Garden of Gethsemane, a place well known to Jesus, a place to which he had come many times before.

Read Luke 22:39-40.

He came out and went, as was his custom, to the Mount of Olives; and the disciples followed him. ⁴⁰ When he reached the place, he said to them, "Pray that you may not come into the time of trial."

This passage comes from the passion of Christ, that time period between the Last Supper and the Crucifixion. The disciples had bonded with Jesus in a different way as they celebrated what would be their last meal together. They wanted to follow Jesus wherever he might go, but they were not yet sure where this path would lead. They had experienced so much with Jesus—miracles, healings, teachings, and confrontations—and they didn't want to miss out on what would come. Yet during their meal, Jesus had told them that he would be betrayed—by one of their own group!

Despite all of the things Jesus had taught them, the disciples still didn't understand his kingdom. They argued among themselves about which one would be the greatest in that kingdom. With all that Jesus had on his mind, he didn't need for his disciples to be squabbling! Peter had claimed to be ready to follow Jesus to prison or even to die with him, but Jesus knew better. Jesus told Peter that he would betray Jesus three times that very night.

Jesus had previously told his followers not to worry about their physical needs when they went from place to place. But now, Jesus has told them that they will need money, provisions, and even something with which to defend themselves! They had two swords with them. Perhaps they thought they were going to begin the rebellion, although a rebellion with two swords would have been pretty short-lived.

With all of these issues weighing on their minds, the disciples (with the exception of Judas) followed Jesus into the garden. Given the mounting tensions surrounding Jesus and his ministry, and Jesus' own prediction of betrayal, the disciples were probably looking for anything that might be awry as they entered the walled garden.

In what observances are Christians expected to participate? Why?

What causes you not to want to miss out on what is to come in journey with Christ?

What things are weighing on your heart and mind? Consider sharing those concerns with your group and asking them to pray with you.

When have you been prepared for a fight and God has said to pray instead? How difficult is it for you to take a step away from stressful times in order to pray?

When Jesus led the disciples into the relative seclusion of the garden, his counsel to pray was a surprise. Isn't that often the case in our own lives? Things get intense, fast paced, and overwhelming. We feel the need to be on the defensive, or maybe even on the attack. Then we get the advice that we really don't want to hear: "Pray about it."

Jesus called the disciples to pray that they might not come into a time of trial or temptation. While I think that's a great idea, I'm struck by the fact that Jesus didn't name the trial or temptation they were to avoid. That's part of the trouble with temptation. It can take many forms and find many avenues. Its point is to add confusion. In fact, "let us not fall into confusion" might be a good way of getting at the root of this prayer. They were to pray that they would not be tempted to step off the path God had placed before them.

Read Luke 22:41-42.

Then he withdrew from them about a stone's throw, knelt down, and prayed, 42 "Father, if you are willing, remove this cup from me; yet, not my will but yours be done."

Jesus moved a few yards away from them and began to pray as well. He didn't just tell the disciples what to do; he followed his own advice. He knew that the times ahead would be horribly painful and miserable. He could have called down angels and gone back to heaven, but he did not. Instead he put his knees in the hard-packed dirt and prayed the most simple, yet profound, prayer: Not my will, but yours be done.

Scenic Route

Jesus humbly kneeled before God and turned himself over completely to God's care. What a strong message. If Jesus, fully man, fully God, needed to rely on God's will, how much more do we? Jesus, completely aware of what was going on, of what would happen, with eyes wide open, asked for God's will to be done.

This prayer is one I have heard from pulpits most of my life, and it sounded good coming from those pulpits. But there are other times when it doesn't sound so good. Sitting in hospital rooms with dying parents, those words are painful to say. Standing in the Neonatal Intensive Care Unit looking at your baby who was born eight weeks early, those words are hard to utter. Seeing the acts of man's inhumanity to man everyday on our news, those words can seem impossible. And yet, those are the moments when we need to pray them the most.

In the darkest of times we need to be reminded that God's will is much bigger than our circumstances. God's will may not lead us down the road we *want* to walk, but it will take us where we *need* to walk.

What do the words not my will, but yours be done mean to you? Why do you think Jesus spoke these words? How willing are you to speak these words?

Where might God be needing you to walk?

Jesus faced the trials ahead of him with his eyes wide open—open to the pain and struggles, but also open to the knowledge that God's will was being done. God's desire to draw all persons into relationship, into new birth, into freedom, was being worked out in each step.

Jesus had asked the disciples to pray essentially the same prayer he had prayed. This prayer was for their preparation as well as his. And yet, when he returned, he found them in a very different posture.

Read Luke 22:45-46.

When he got up from prayer, he came to the disciples and found them sleeping because of grief, [46] *and he said to them, "Why are you sleeping? Get up and pray that you may not come into the time of trial."*

Jesus found the disciples asleep on the job! Instead of keeping their eyes open, they shut them, and by shutting them they were lulled to sleep. When I picture this scene, I often think of a youth reenactment of this scene that I once saw. They young man playing Jesus returned and found all of the disciples asleep. He yelled at them to keep awake, but one disciple still didn't sit up. Then the Jesus character kicked the still sleeping disciple to wake him.

Sometimes I feel like I need a kick to remember what I'm supposed to be doing. It can be far too easy to be lulled to sleep by my grief. There is so much to grieve. If I sit there with my grief long enough, I can get overwhelmed. I can begin to feel like nothing can change it and that certainly nothing I do can be of any help.

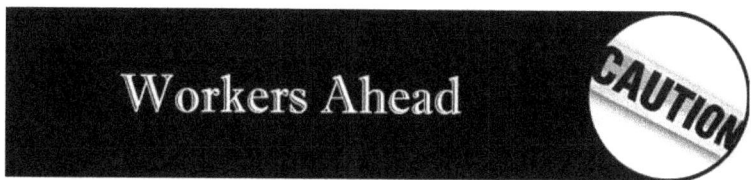

Workers Ahead CAUTION

Keeping our eyes open even in the midst of all of the suffering and grief in the world is very important. We cannot walk through our lives like sleepwalkers, hoping against hope that we will awaken from this nightmare and be in a new heaven and a new earth. We cannot stay asleep to the needs of those around us because it hurts too much to see them.

As the people of God, we must keep awake and not ignore earthly suffering because God has promised healing and wholeness "one day." We are called to enter into the world and to live in the reality that God is present with us now; that God's will is being worked out even in the middle of the agony we see.

Asking for God's will to be done does not imply giving up and letting things fall where they may. Jesus actively participated in the last several hours of his life, knowing that people for centuries to come would remember and reflect on those moments, gaining strength for their own times of trial. Jesus participated with God in bringing about God's will on earth.

What trials are you experiencing right now? How can you see God's will being done? What about trials of the past? How have you seen God's will emerge from the darkness?

When has grief overwhelmed you? In what situations have you struggled to stay awake, alert to God's will?

How do you respond to the issues of violence and suffering in the world? How does your faith community respond?

How does your faith community make people's needs known? How do you go about meeting those needs?

God calls us to be alert to what is going on around us so that we might not fall into the time of trial. By opening our eyes to the needs and concerns of those around us, we become better able to love others as Christ loves us, wholly and completely.

As a group, look around your faith community. Who is in need? How can you help them? Even something as simple as offering a cool drink of water can be God's will because it may offer hope during a dark time. Look around your local community. To whom can your community of faith reach out with offers of hope, love, warmth, acceptance, and grace? How can you enter into such a ministry?

In the Rear View

Jesus' prayer in the garden was so simple, so short. Yet in it we find so much strength and hope. Asking for God's will to be done allows us to get unstuck from the inward focus we so easily develop and begin to look once more at others, whom we are also called to love.

Join together with others in your group as you pray:

Lord God, thank you for your example of prayer. Thank you for keeping your eyes open to the suffering of the world you came to save. Grant us the ability to keep our eyes open to this world you love so much. Let us become aware of your will in our lives. Help us to see where you are working and give us the strength to join in that work. Keep us from the temptations we face—the temptation to give up, to turn our backs to the needs of others. Give us open eyes, open hearts, and open arms. In the name of Christ we pray. Amen.

Travel Log

Day 1:

Read again the stanza of "Sweet Hour of Prayer" from the beginning of this lesson. Where in your life do you need relief? Where do you find your hope? Journal your thoughts as you reflect on the questions.

Day 2:

Jesus took his disciples away to pray, which he did fairly often. Where do you go to get away and pray? What space have you set aside for spending time in prayer with God? Sketch a simple drawing of your ideal place to pray.

Day 3:

How have you let your eyes be closed by grief? What other options are available? How might you acknowledge your grief, but remember to have hope?

Using the space below, list the ways you can acknowledge your grief. Also list the hope that you have found in the midst of your grief.

Day 4:

Be alert today. Keep your eyes open and your ears ready. Take notes of things that you hear, prayer requests, needs, praises, joys. Write them down and offer them to God as your prayer today.

Day 5:

If your church has a prayer list, take time today to ask God's will to be done in each person's situation. Pray as specifically as you can for God's will, asking the Holy Spirit to help you. If your church does not have a prayer list, create one of your own. Write down each need and then periodically review to see how God is answering the prayers.

Day 6:

Times of trial and temptation are different for us all. What is the temptation you face the most today? How is God equipping you to face that temptation? Jot down some words that will help you to face the temptation.

Day 7:

Luke's account of the prayer at the Mount of Olives shows us Jesus at perhaps his most human, asking for the cup to pass. When have you asked for the same thing? When have you been delivered? When have you had to continue on the path? What good came out of that situation? Who stood with you during those times?

Write a note of appreciation to the people who helped you to find God's will in the midst of these situations.